This book is based upon LIVING ARCTIC: HUNTERS OF
THE CANADIAN NORTH, a temporary exhibition supported
by Indigenous Survival International at the Museum of
Mankind (the Ethnography Department of the British
Museum) 1987-89.

The author and publishers would like to thank the
Education Service and the Department of Ethnography
of the British Museum for their help in the preparation
of this book.
They would also like to thank Bernardine Murphy
Headteacher of Our Lady Queen of Heaven R.C. First
School, the children in class 4.2, their parents and their
class teacher, Ann Ramiz, as well as Jenny Beard, Jan
Bradley and Bobby Hurdman for their participation.

The author and publishers would like to thank the following for
supplying additional photographs for this book:

Title page	(*Inuit children*) © B & C Alexander
Page 14	(*Dene at summer camp*) © Fran Huncomb/Department of Culture and Communications, North West Territories Government
Page 15	(*Village, Resolute Bay, N.W.T., Canda*) © Arctic Camera
Page 15	(*School, Cambridge Bay, N.W.T., Canada*) © Tessa Macintosh/Department of Culture and Communication, N.W.T. Government.
Page 21	(*Inuit with Skidoo*) © B & C Alexander

OUR ARCTIC PROJECT

Ruth Thomson

Photographs by Neil Thomson

Hamish Hamilton

London

Snow goose

Snowy owl

Puffins

This term our class is doing a project about the cold lands of the Arctic. The Arctic is the area around the North Pole. The land is covered with snow and ice for most of the year, and the sea freezes over in winter.

Mrs Ramiz has brought lots of library books for us to read, so that we can find out what lives in the Arctic. We each choose a different animal or bird to paint, and use our pictures to decorate our classroom.

Peter decides to paint a polar bear. He makes it look very fierce indeed. Polar bears are very good hunters. Their white fur makes them hard to see against the snow. They can kill seals with just a swipe of their powerful paws.

Stuart and Natalie paint the head of a seal coming up through a hole in the ice. In the Arctic seals live in the sea under the ice. They make holes so that they can come up to breathe.

'Do any people live in the Arctic?' asked Mrs Ramiz.
'Yes,' says Richard, 'the Eskimos.'

'The Eskimos prefer to be called the Inuit now,' says Mrs
Ramiz. 'This is the name they call themselves. It means "the
people". The Inuit and other people from the Candian Arctic
have helped to set up an exhibition to show how they live.
Tomorrow we are going to a museum to see it.'

Everyone is very excited about going on an outing.

When we go into the museum, we see the model of an Inuit man dressed in furs, in the entrance hall.

LIVING
ARCTIC
HUNTERS OF THE CANADIAN-NORTH

'He must be rather hot wearing those clothes in here,' jokes Michael.

'But he would be glad of them when it's 30°C below zero, in an arctic winter,' smiles Mrs Ramiz.

Shawn, the museum teacher, leads us into the exhibition.

'I want you to pretend you are researchers, finding out about who lives in the Arctic and what their life is like.'

The way in is dimly lit. The walls around us are blue and we can hear a low whistling wind. It makes us feel chilly. We shiver a little to think what it would be like in the Arctic.

'Did you know that there are two areas of the Arctic?' says Shawn, showing us a big map. 'In the high Arctic it is too cold for trees to grow. In the Subarctic, there are plenty of trees.'

He points to the map and asks us who lives in the high Arctic. We all put up our hands.
'The Inuit,' says Laura.
'Other groups of people live in the Subarctic,' says Shawn. 'Two are called the Cree and the Dene.'

Shawn takes us to look at the tent where the Cree sometimes live when they are out hunting.

When we peer inside, we can see bedding rolls and a fireplace made of stones.
'I wonder why they live in tents?' says Toni-Marie. We try to work out what makes a tent a good place to live in when they are out hunting.

Everyone jostles to have a look
through the doorway of a log cabin.

'The Dene and the Cree live in cabins
like this when they are out hunting in
the winter,' Shawn explains. 'It can
be very cold, but the men still go out
to check the traps.'

Shawn asks us what this kind of home is called. That's an
easy question.

'An igloo,' choruses everybody.

'Wrong,' says Shawn. 'Igloo is the Inuit word for any kind of
home, so that means that you all live in igloos too! The Inuit
call this a snowhouse. They do not live in them any more,
but they sometimes use them when they are out hunting.'

'The Inuit live in wooden homes like this now,' says Shawn. Inside there's a computer and a TV, and the food cupboards are filled with packets of cereals, dried milk and tinned foods. We notice a lot of other things that we have in our homes. But some things are different, like the seal skins.

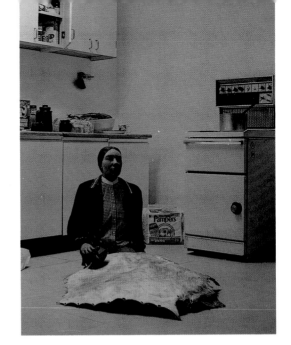

Shawn tells us that the houses are shipped ready-made from southern Canada in the summer, when the sea ice has melted.

A snowmobile is parked outside the house. Everyone wants a turn on it. 'It must be fun whizzing across the ice at top speed,' says Sonia.

'But what if it breaks down on a freezing cold day?' asks Katie.

'Anyone who uses one needs to be a good mechanic,' says Shawn. 'Otherwise he could be stranded miles from home. Dogs are more reliable, even if they don't go as fast.'

We also have a look at the buggy, which the Inuit use in summer. It has enormous wheels for going over bumpy ground. There are no roads outside the towns in the Arctic; people can drive wherever it is safe. But buggies can damage the plants and so some people don't like them.

Shawn takes us into the activity room to tell us more about the people who live in the Arctic. He shows us some slides.

'Is there anything surprising about this slide?' he asks.
'There's no snow,' says Simon.
'That's right,' agrees Shawn. 'The snow melts in summer. This is very important.

If snow covered the ground all year round there would be no plants and insects. If there were no plants and insects to eat, there would be no animals on land. Without these animals to hunt, people would find it hard to live there.'

The school looks quite similar to ours.

'Look, they've got pictures of arctic animals on the wall, just like we have,' says Marie.

'What is different about an arctic village from where you live?' asks Shawn.

'There are no trees or gardens,' says Giles.

'Tell me,' says Shawn, 'You saw that the Inuit have things in their houses, which they buy just like your families do. You saw that the Dene wear jeans and have rifles and cooking pots which they must buy. Where do you think they get their money from? What have they got to sell?'

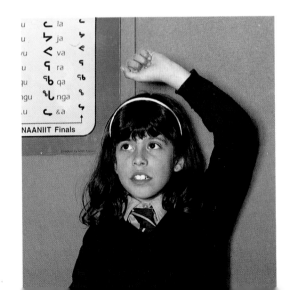

'Skins,' answers Juanita.
'They also sell their craft work,' says Shawn. 'And the government sometimes gives them money.'

We find out how the Dene hunt for caribou, a kind of reindeer.

They hunt them on foot. They wear jeans and a jacket – even in cold weather, because tracking animals is hot work. When they stop moving they make a fire to keep warm. On their feet they wear soft leather moccasins, which make no noise. In winter, they wear snowshoes so that they do not sink into the deep snow. They use rifles as their weapons.

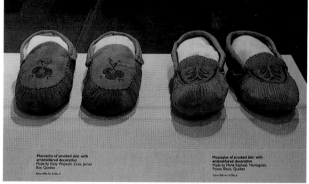

Moccasins of smoked skin with embroidered decoration
Made by Kitty Wapachii, Cree, James Bay, Quebec

Moccasins of smoked skin with embroidered decoration
Made by Marie Raphael, Montagnais, Pointe Bleue, Quebec

Some of us pretend to be a herd of caribou. Shawn puts a real caribou skin over Simon. It is so enormous, it would cover at least two of us completely!

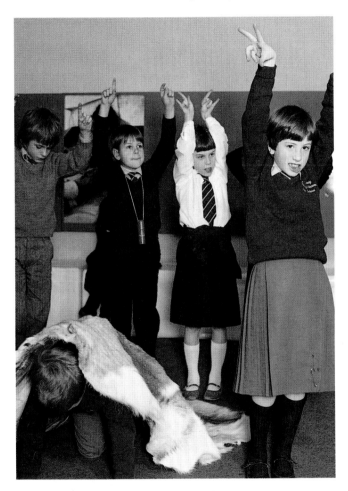

The Dene hunter is very skilful. He could shoot as many caribou as he wants. But he does not. He shoots only one. It is all the food that he needs and all he can carry. He puts it on a sledge to take home.

Shawn gives Katie a pair of caribou socks to try on. The Inuit need to dress very warmly for hunting. They wear clothes of fur or modern fabrics. When they hunt for seals, they may have to wait all day at a breathing hole, and if they aren't moving they can get very cold.

Everyone laughs with Katie. The socks are so long!

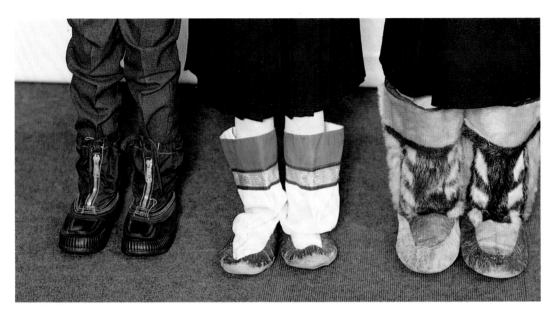

The Inuit wear all sorts of boots. We try some on.

'A skilled woman can make a pair of sealskin boots that are completely waterproof,' says Shawn.

The boots are sewn with the sinew from a caribou. Shawn holds some sinew along his back to show us where the sinew comes from. It makes good strong thread. Sometimes the Inuit decorate their boots with patterns. Each village has its own patterns. If they are travelling by snowmobile, they sometimes wear boots with rubber soles and plastic tops.

The Inuit's outer clothes may be made of animal furs. They are much warmer for the cold winters than any other kind of clothing. We all have a turn feeling a pair of caribou gloves. Helen is surprised by their smell.

Today many Inuit also wear clothes made of cloth instead of furs.

Back at school, we make some of the things we saw at the museum. Sonia and Tracey are making a log cabin. When the Dene and the Cree make log cabins they cover the roof with lichen and moss. Ours has snow made of cotton wool on top.

'Sometimes the log cabins are miles from anywhere,' says Sonia. 'What happens if someone is ill and needs help?'

'I expect they send a message by radio,' says Tracey. 'That's how they keep in touch with other people.'

We write our own dance drama about the Arctic, to share what we have learned with the rest of the school.

We make animal masks to wear. Michael is a polar bear. Christopher is a walrus.

The musicians play drums and tambourines. John reads the story we have made up about an Inuit hunting expedition.

'The Inuit live in the Arctic. They hunt seals, walrus and other animals.

They respect animals and their land. They are not greedy. They never kill more animals than they need. They don't waste anything and they look after the land and animals for the future.

They know that if they killed too many, the animals could
become extinct. People in the Arctic believe that the land and
the food should be shared with everyone. It is a good way to
live.

Inuit hunters often search for many hours. When they find a
walrus they creep up on it very quietly. One of the hunters
throws a sharp harpoon. Everyone helps to haul the walrus
out of the water, because it is heavy.'

At the end of our drama everyone claps. Then they come to
see the display we have made during our Arctic project. We
tell them all about our visit to the museum and everything we
saw there.

HAMISH HAMILTON CHILDREN'S BOOKS

Published by the Penguin Group
27 Wrights Lane, London W8 5TZ, England
Viking Penguin Inc, 40 West 23rd Street, New York, New York 10010, U.S.A.
Penguin Books Australia Ltd, Ringwood, Victoria, Australia
Penguin Books Canada Ltd, 2801 John Street, Markham, Ontario, Canada L3R 1B4
Penguin Books (N.Z.) Ltd, 182-190 Wairau Road, Auckland 10, New Zealand

Penguin Books Ltd, Registered Offices: Harmondsworth, Middlesex, England

First published in Great Britain 1989 by
Hamish Hamilton Children's Books

Text copyright © 1989 by Ruth Thomson
Photographs copyright © 1989 by Neil Thomson
Design by Tony Garrett

1 3 5 7 9 10 8 6 4 2

British Library Cataloguing in Publication Data

Thomson, Ruth, *1949-*
Our Arctic project.
1. Arctic. Animals – For children
I. Title
591.998

ISBN 0-241-12633-9

Printed in Singapore